Teenage Refugees From

BOSNIA-HERZEGOVINA

Speak Out

BEFORE THE WAR

HUNGARY

SLOVENIA

ROMANIA

CROATIA

YUGOSLAVIA

Banja Luka

Bihac

SERBIA

BOSNIA-
HERZEGOVINA

Sarajevo

Mostar

Adriatic Sea

MONTENEGRO

☐ Yugoslavia

ALBANIA

MACEDONIA

(Above) Before the outbreak of civil war in 1991, Bosnia-Herzegovina was a republic of Yugoslavia.
(Below) Under the 1995 peace agreement, the newly independent Bosnia-Herzegovina remains a single
country, but is now divided into two parts: the Bosnian-Croat Federation and the Bosnian Serb Republic.

AFTER THE WAR

CROATIA

Bihac

Banja Luka

Brcko

BOSNIA-
HERZEGOVINA

SERBIA

Sarajevo

Gorazde

Adriatic Sea

Mostar

YUGOSLAVIA

☐ Bosnian-Croat Federation

MONTENEGRO

☐ Bosnian Serb Republic

IN THEIR OWN VOICES

Teenage Refugees From
BOSNIA-
HERZEGOVINA
Speak Out

VALERIE TEKAVEC

THE ROSEN PUBLISHING GROUP, INC.
NEW YORK

Published in 1995, 1997 by The Rosen Publishing Group, Inc.
29 East 21st Street, New York, NY 10010

Revised Edition 1997

Copyright © 1995, 1997 by The Rosen Publishing Group, Inc.

Manufactured in the United States of America.

Library of Congress Cataloging-in-Publication Data

Teenage refugees from Bosnia-Herzegovina speak out / Valerie Tekavec.— rev. ed.
   p.   cm.— (In their own voices)
Includes bibliographical references and index.
ISBN 0-8239-2560-9
  1. Bosnian American teenagers—Juvenile literature. 2. Refugees—United States—Juvenile literature. [Bosnian Americans. 2. Refugees. 3. Youths' writings.] I. Tekavec, Valerie. II. Series.
E184.B67T45 1995
305.23'5'0899182073—dc20   94-40369
                                           CIP
                                           AC

Contents

Smoke rises over the city of Sarajevo in early 1994 after heavy shelling forced residents to remain indoors.

INTRODUCTION

Yugoslavia, located in southeastern Europe, was once a nation of six republics: Bosnia-Herzegovina, Croatia, Macedonia, Montenegro, Serbia, and Slovenia. On June 25, 1991, civil war broke out after Croatia and Slovenia voted to secede, or break away, from Yugoslavia and become independent states. The war spread to Bosnia-Herzegovina when it declared independence on February 29, 1992. The fighting was mainly between Yugoslavia's three major ethnic groups: Croats, Muslims, and Serbs.

Ethnic diversity is one of the defining features of Bosnia-Herzegovina. In 1991, Bosnia-Herzegovina was home to approximately 4.3 million people, including Albanians, Bulgarians, Croats, Hungarians, Jews, Macedonians, Montenegrins, Muslims, Serbs, Slovaks, and Slovenes. Within this population, approximately 44 percent were Muslim, 31 percent Serb, and 17 percent Croat. The teenagers you will read about in this book each belong to one of these three ethnic groups. All are victims of the problems that can occur when ethnic and religious tolerance breaks down in a society.

Croats, Muslims, and Serbs are part of a larger European ethnic group called South Slavs. They all descended from a common set of Slavic ancestors who migrated south from the plains of Europe into Bosnia 1,400 years ago. How then did the Croats, Muslims, and Serbs of Bosnia, who share exactly the same ancestors, become such bitter enemies? There is no simple answer to this question, but looking at their history is a good way to begin understanding their recent conflict.

Bosnia has often been invaded and ruled by foreigners. Each foreign power influenced the politics, culture, and way of life of the Bosnians. Over time, cultural and religious differences developed among Bosnians.

Religion is a key difference between Croats, Muslims, and Serbs. A division within the Christian Church developed in the ninth century. It was called the Great Schism. By 1054, it had resulted in the division between the Roman Catholic and Eastern Orthodox Churches. The line dividing these two camps ran through the region that is present-day Bosnia-Herzegovina. Those who lived on the west side of the dividing line—the Croats—became Roman Catholic, while those to the east—the Serbs—became Eastern Orthodox. Islam—the religion of the Muslims—was brought into the region during the Ottoman invasions in the fifteenth century.

Bosnia was conquered by the Ottoman Turks in 1463, becoming a part of the Ottoman Empire.

After nearly four years of civil war, a peace agreement was signed by Serbian President Slobodan Milosevic (left), Croatian President Franjo Tudjman (center), and Bosnian President Alija Izetbegovic (right) on December 14, 1995, in Paris.

Its neighbor, Herzegovina, fell to the Turks in 1482 and was joined with Bosnia to form Bosnia-Herzegovina. Under Turkish rule, some Bosnians converted to Islam in exchange for freedom, jobs, and land. However, these Muslims continued to identify themselves as Slavs.

The power of the Ottoman Empire declined and Bosnia-Herzegovina came under the control of the Austro-Hungarian Empire in 1878. Frustrated by centuries of foreign rule, many Slavs rallied behind the idea of forming a unified, self-ruled nation of Yugoslavs, or South Slavs. Austria-Hungary tried to crush the movement for Slavic independence.

In 1914, a Serb patriot assassinated the Archduke of Austria-Hungary who was visiting

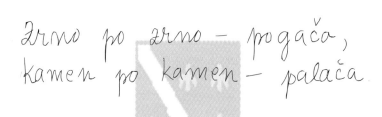

Zrno po zrno – pogača,
kamen po kamen – palača.

ENGLISH TRANSLATION FROM SERBO-CROATIAN:
Grain by grain—a loaf of bread,
stone by stone—a house is made.

Sarajevo, the Bosnian capital. This act sparked World War I. By the end of the war, the Austro-Hungarian Empire collapsed. Yugoslavia emerged as an independent country in 1918.

During World War II, Germany's Nazi forces invaded Yugoslavia. While the Yugoslav army fought the Germans, a Croatian pro-Nazi organization, the Ustashe, sided with the Nazis. Together, the Ustashe and the Nazis murdered Jews and hundreds of thousands of Serbs in Croatia and Bosnia-Herzegovina. The willingness of many Croats to kill their neigbors has haunted Serbs ever since. It partly explains the hostility between Croats and Serbs in the recent civil war.

Josip Broz Tito led the resistance army that freed Yugoslavia from Nazi occupation forces. Near the end of World War II, he was elected Prime Minister and set up a Communist government. In 1946, Bosnia-Herzegovina became one of the six republics of Yugoslavia.

Yugoslavia was intended to be a federation in which different ethnicities could live together peacefully, despite their differences. Ruling with charisma and an iron fist, Tito led his diverse peoples toward the goal of an ethnically tolerant state.

The thread holding Yugoslavia's ethnic groups together began to unravel after Tito's death in 1980. Tensions resurfaced between the ethnic groups of Yugoslavia. When communism began to collapse throughout Eastern Europe in 1989, nationalist movements emerged in some Yugoslavian republics.

These movements led to the outbreak of civil war. In 1991, Croatia declared its independence. The Serb minority in Croatia rebelled. These Serb rebels, remembering the Croats' treatment of Serbs in World War II, were afraid of being treated unfairly in the newly created Croatian state.

Meanwhile, in Bosnia-Herzegovina, Muslims and Croats, who together made a majority, voted in 1992 to create an independent country. They feared that Serbs would dominate what remained of Yugoslavia. But Bosnian Serbs didn't want to become a minority in the new Bosnia-Herzegovina. Supported by the Serb-dominated Yugoslav army, they began a military rebellion against Bosnian independence.

Each ethnic group wanted to expand its territory or to reclaim land that had once belonged to it. Croats, Muslims, and Serbs all attempted to carve out areas of Bosnia-Herzegovina for themselves by forcibly removing other ethnic groups. This policy was known as "ethnic cleansing."

The tactics used by Croats, Muslims, and Serbs were horrific in their cruelty and disregard for human life. Prisoners were put in concentration camps. Some were starved, tortured, raped, and executed. Muslims, Croats, and Serbs alike experienced these atrocities.

As the conflict raged on, the international community struggled with a difficult question: Should it become directly involved in the conflict or leave it to be resolved by the warring parties themselves? The United Nations sent peacekeepers to the former Yugoslavia in 1992, but was unable to fulfill its mission. Peace did not seem possible until the United States led a diplomatic effort, supported by the military alliance called NATO (North Atlantic Treaty Organization), to stop the fighting.

On November 21, 1995, a peace agreement was reached in Dayton, Ohio, by the presidents of the former republics of Serbia, Croatia, and Bosnia-Herzegovina. According to the conditions of the agreement, Bosnia-Herzegovina remains a single country, but is now divided into two parts: the Bosnian-Croat Federation, shared reluctantly by Croats and Muslims, and the Bosnian Serb Republic. An international military force is stationed in Bosnia-Herzegovina to maintain peace.

The fighting has finally stopped, but there are still many problems to be solved. The Yugoslav conflict has left a bitter legacy in Bosnia-Herzegovina. An estimated 200,000 people are dead, many of them children. The same number of people have been injured. Approximately 2.7 million Bosnians were forced to leave their native country. Many of these refugees no longer have homes to which they can return. Countless cities and towns lie in ruins.

Looking beyond these grim statistics and seeing the faces they represent will help you to understand the tragedy of Bosnia-Herzegovina. The eight teenage refugees in the book emigrated from Bosnia-Herzegovina to North America to escape danger and persecution. They were forced to leave behind their homes, family, friends, and cultural ties. In facing this traumatic experience of separation, the teenagers profiled in this book have shown great courage.

*　　　　*　　　　*

Some of the teenagers interviewed for this book asked that their photographs not be used. In most cases, only the students' first names have been used in order to protect their privacy.◆

Enisa is a young poet. Her poems have been published in Serbo-Croat and in French translation.

Enisa is very close to her family. Her story shows how, in the face of complete loss, family is what matters most.

When Enisa arrived in New York City in August 1993, 200,000 people had already died in the war in Bosnia. She talks about the death of her generation and how it will affect the country and her city, Sarajevo.

To My Generation by Enisa Begic
Silence and peace in schools,
Dust and shame in a street,
Who is going to the prom
With dead graduates?

Their dreams, words and happiness
Have ended too early,
The ones from the mountain
Struck youth of Sarajevo,
Wounded it and took its joy.

I am slowly wandering around Sarajevo
Looking at the dusty, flat field;
A school was once here,
Neither school nor half of students
Are here now.

I feel tears rolling down my face,
I am trying to see the cowards
Who killed youth of 'my' city,
Where so many children were lost
Without any trace.

ENISA
LIFE IN SARAJEVO

I had a wonderful life in Sarajevo before the war broke out. My school and teachers were great. My parents had good jobs. I had everything I wished for.

Religion and nationality were not important to my parents and me. What was important was that people were good. I never even knew if some of my friends were Serbs or Croats. I didn't want to know. I still love them, and I know they're not responsible for what has happened. My best friend is a Croat, but she identifies herself as a Bosnian.

I lived in Ilidza, a part of Sarajevo where many Serbs lived. I am Muslim. Everything was peaceful between us, but when the war started, Serbs changed. They didn't want to talk to me or come to my house anymore. Many Serbs started sending their children away to Serbia. School was

Two Bosnian students prepare for school to open again. Their school was renamed for a teacher who was killed during an attack by Serb forces.

going to start in a few days, and all the children were gone. I looked around my empty neighborhood and asked myself, "Why?"

The day I left Sarajevo, I felt I was looking at it for the last time. I went with my father and my sister to Trogir, a town in Croatia near Split. My mother stayed behind to work as a nurse in a mobile unit in Ilidza. Ten days later, the doctor told my mother and the staff that they shouldn't come to the unit anymore because they might be taken hostage.

There were Serb nationalists everywhere. My mother often heard shots being fired. The principal of my elementary school, a Muslim, was killed by the gym teacher of the same school. My mother came to Croatia on the last train to leave Sarajevo. After that, the station was burned.

In those ten days before she came to Croatia, I found out what "mother" means. My sister and I cried the whole time. When she finally made it to Trogir, I was very happy.

I finished my last year of high school in Croatia. When my mother went to enroll me, the school principal asked, "What is your religion?" When she told him that we were Muslim, he said, "We have no place for Muslims."

My mother didn't want to tell me about what the principal had said. She just told me that I might have difficulty getting into that school. But then we met a great man who was a teacher at the school. When he saw my school records from Bosnia, he said he would do everything he could to get me into the school.

I was so heartbroken in Croatia. I felt like an old woman. I didn't go anywhere. I only had a few friends I saw at school. I watched the news all day and cried. I dreamed of my house and my Sarajevo.

So many young people have died in Sarajevo. Sometimes I ask myself, "How did this happen? How did my friends, Muslims, Serbs, and Croats take sides and start killing each other?"

In the weeks before we left Croatia, I heard people saying bad things about Muslims all the time. It was very upsetting. On the airplane, the flight attendants were so nice to me. As we were getting off the plane, they started to cry. When that happened I thought, "I will love America, and America is going to love me." It was an important moment for me. I'll never forget it.

We had a series of interviews with the United Nations office in Croatia before we came to New York. The immigration office found an apartment for us and gave us $480 for food; that was supposed to last us two months. There was no furniture. They told us to sleep on the floor. All we had were our bags. We had no money, nothing. It was like starting over again.

We have been lucky to meet some people from Bosnia who have lived here for years. They helped us find a better apartment and even helped us get furniture. I love New York City and I'm very happy to be here. I feel different here. I am stronger.

Sometimes I lose hope that I will ever go back to Bosnia. But then I think, how stupid and terrible of me. There are people fighting and dying in Sarajevo, and here I am losing hope. I know it won't be the same when I go back.

My friends write to me from all over the world. They are refugees, too. They all say, "We will go back someday to Sarajevo." I know we will return and we will rebuild our Sarajevo and our Bosnia.◆

Josip Broz Tito served as prime minister of Yugoslavia for 35 years, after establishing a Communist government there near the end of World War II.

Ljubica is a Serbian refugee living in Virginia. Ljubica is a bright, energetic girl who has managed to support herself and go to school entirely alone in the United States. The rest of her family is still in Bosnia.

She talks a lot about the American media and their coverage of the war in Bosnia. Her views are penetrating and insightful. She believes that the Serbs as a group are portrayed negatively.

Ljubica also struggles with national prejudice. Coming from a place filled with rage, she tries not to fall into long-established patterns of hatred between the national groups. She is very honest about how it affects her internally, but she also believes it is necessary to retain one's identity.

LJUBICA
WHAT AM I?

My name is Ljubica. I had just turned 18 when I came to the United States. I am from a small town not far from Banja Luka. I came to the U.S. as an exchange student, and I lived with a family in a little town outside Philadelphia.

I went to high school there for a year. The first four months were nice. I was meeting people, making friends. I was a normal teenager, I guess. But I wasn't happy with many things in America. It's not easy to make good friends here. I mostly made friends with other exchange students.

Then the war broke out. I remember talking to my dad on the phone in the spring. I asked him if anything was going on in my town, and he said, "No, everything's fine!" But it was close. There was fighting right across the river, on the border between Bosnia and Croatia.

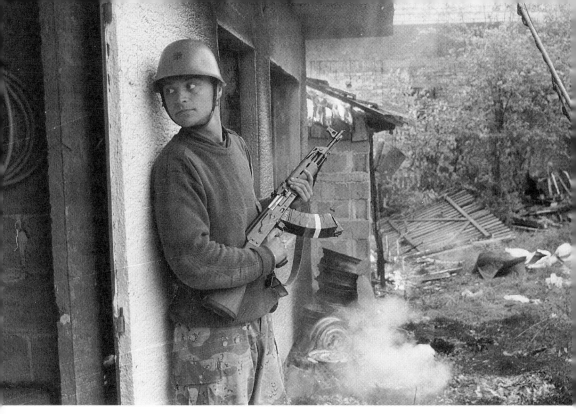

A Serbian soldier takes cover behind a burning house in a Bosnian village.

About a month after we spoke, the phone lines were disconnected, and I knew that they were in the war. I was unable to contact my family from April to September in 1992.

My exchange year in the U.S. was coming to a close, and when it was time for me to leave, I didn't know where to go. So I applied for political asylum in the U.S. I got my employment authorization. A month later, I got a job as a nanny. I worked for a couple in Philadelphia with two little kids. Then I moved with them to Washington, D.C. All this time I didn't know anything about my parents. It was the worst five months of my life.

I remember my 19th birthday, in July. I was

writing a letter to my parents. I wrote to my old

address, although I didn't know if it would get through. It was a very emotional letter. I cried all over it. The paper was wet.

My parents got the letter at the end of August, two days before my father had to go to the front lines to fight. They read it and cried. Dad said he would go to the front and fight once more, and when he came back he would get right into the car and go get me. But he was wounded. It was a miracle that he survived.

My father is committed to staying in Bosnia. I hope to go back, too. But now I'm going to a community college in Falls Church, Virginia. I'm doing general studies. I plan to stay in the U.S. until I finish a four-year degree somewhere.

My people have a lot to offer me. We have a very rich culture. We're very intelligent people. And we're very good-hearted, even though we're getting this bad rap right now. We have children, we love our children. We go to church, we listen to music. We are people, but we're being portrayed as animals.

Now, when people say Bosnia is this multi-cultural country where everybody got along, it's a huge lie. You always knew who was a Muslim, who was a Serb, who was a Croat. And you got along nicely as long as you didn't marry them. It's the same as the Jewish-Catholic thing here. I'm not saying it's right, but that's the way it is. What's happening in Bosnia is going on in other places in the world. It got violent in my country, but the violence could happen anywhere else, too.

It's been very hard for me and my Bosnian friends living here in the United States. When you say, "I'm from Yugoslavia," the question, "From what part of Yugoslavia?" always follows. When you answer, "Bosnia," the person says, "Oh! What are you?" When I answer, "Serbian," people say things like, "Oh! You're the bad guys!"

This has happened to me hundreds of times. People condemn the whole nation for something they don't even know about. Like the 60,000 rapes: A report by the United Nations states that a total of 800 rapes occurred in Bosnia, 350 of which they have evidence for. It also states that all sides had an equal part in it.

People in Bosnia are dying, and it's very bad. But people overlook that people in Serbia are dying, too. Children are dying because of the sanctions. People don't have food, basic medical supplies. I don't understand the purpose for cutting them off. Sometimes, I think, "I'm so sick of the words 'Muslim,' 'Serbian,' 'Croatian,' 'NATO.'" That's my life, the war. It's not very pleasant. The bookshelves in my room are lined with books like *The State of Croatia* or *The Serbs.*

I still hang out with a lot of Yugoslavians. We get into discussions sometimes and we argue. If

Many refugees who were displaced by the war have no home to which they can return. Above is a Serb refugee who returned to the town of Sipovo, only to find his house reduced to a heap of rubble.

somebody says the Serbs are the ones who are doing all the killing, I get very mad. But if someone says everyone is a victim, you have your goal, we have ours, I react pretty calmly. I can see that I'm talking to a rational person. I'm not a crazy nationalist. I believe that it's fine to be proud of who you are, as long as you don't intrude on anyone else's national feelings.

I think American kids should try to overcome their ignorance. They should read about Bosnian history, like Ivo Andric's book *The Bridge on the Drina.* People should learn something about Bosnia and the Serbs before they hang them.◆

Alexander is thirteen years old. He is a Croat and comes from a town that had a mainly Croat population. When he first left his country, he was a refugee in Croatia. Many Bosnian-Croats have moved to neighboring Croatia as refugees. Unlike the Muslims, the Croats and Serbs have had "sister countries" to flee to. But it didn't work out in Croatia for Alexander's family and they had to move on. So they came to Canada.

ALEXANDER
LEAVING BIHAC

My name is Alexander. I come from Bihac, a town in northwestern Bosnia-Herzegovina. Bihac is very close to the Croatian border, on the Una River. I live in Toronto, Canada, now. My mother's sister sponsored me and my family to come here. My aunt has been in Canada for six years.

Becoming a refugee was a big change in my life. I came to a new city. I didn't speak English very well, and I didn't have any friends. I've been here for eight months now and have some friends. That makes things a little easier. My new friends are Canadian, Polish, and Chinese.

There was a lot of fighting in Bihac in the war, but I left before it started. There were Serbs, Croats, and Muslims living in my town, but the largest group was Croatian. I am Croatian, too.

The Croatian city of Dubrovnik was shelled by the Yugoslav federal army in 1991.

I left Bihac almost three years ago. At first I lived in Croatia, in Zagreb, with my mother and my sister. We stayed there for two years. It was a very difficult time. My father couldn't come with us. The Serbs in Bosnia wouldn't let him cross the border into Croatia. I still haven't seen my father since we left Bihac, and for a long time it was impossible to reach him by phone or letter.

The last year we spent in Zagreb we had refugee status. We were very hungry. There was no food, no coal, no wood, nothing. Now we are doing much better, and my father will be arriving in Toronto in a few days. I am very excited, because my family will finally be back together again. He was wounded in the war, but he is O.K.

Right now I'm taking ESL at my school. My English is getting better. My favorite subject is math. When I was in Bosnia I liked history, and I used to play soccer and basketball. In Toronto, I like to play ice hockey, but they don't offer soccer at my school. After school I like to watch TV.

When we lived in Bosnia, my mother was a social worker. My father drove a truck. Right now my mother is working at the Croatian Club in Toronto. When I am older, I would like to be a cop.

There are very few Croats living in Bihac now. Many have left the town as refugees and have gone to live in Croatia. I don't think I will ever go back to Bosnia. I will stay in Canada. There is nothing left for me in Bosnia.◆

Jasmin has been in the United States for only a short time. He is Muslim. The journey from his village in western Bosnia to his new home in Utica, New York, took seven months. When Jasmin arrived with his family, they had no home, no jobs, and no knowledge of English. The resettlement agency in Utica helped them find a home in Corn Hill, an old, economically depressed area where 65 percent of the houses are abandoned. The neighborhood is known for its refugee community.

Jasmin is an intense young man. He and his family experienced much physical and emotional strain in Bosnia. Yet, despite the hardship, he maintains an awesome stoicism. His rigid manner and clipped language hint at fresh wounds yet to heal.

JASMIN
NIGHTS IN THE FOREST

My name is Jasmin. I come from Ramic, a village in western Bosnia, near the city of Ključ. My village is a good size. There are 100 houses and three or four roads. Ramic is a very beautiful place. It lies on the slope of a small hill. The country is very green.

I am now here in Utica, New York, with my family. I have a brother and a sister. My grandmother and my uncle live with us, too. I am the oldest child. I am 18.

I arrived as a refugee in the United States a little more than a month ago. When I left Bosnia, I left many friends behind. They are scattered, as refugees, all over the world, in Canada, France, and Germany. Some of them are still in Bosnia, fighting in the war.

I went to elementary school in my village. I was a good student there. I received the highest grades. When I turned 13, I went to another school in a nearby village, Velegici. Later, until the war broke out, I went to school in Ključ, seven kilometers

Sarajevo residents run to avoid sniper fire in the city's infamous "Sniper Alley."

away. I took the bus there every day. My favorite subjects are math, physics, and chemistry. I also like sports, especially soccer.

When the war started, my school was suddenly closed and barricaded. All over Bosnia, people started taking sides. Provocations began in my village, and the Yugoslavian army came in. Certain Muslims in the village killed three soldiers. That is when the trouble really began. After that incident, I, my father, my uncle, and others were arrested. One of the people who arrested us was our next-door neighbor. I was released the following day, but they locked up my father and uncle in a cell in Novo Gradiska. Some days later they were taken to a camp in the city of Banja Luka, where 4,500 people were imprisoned. They held my father and uncle for seven months.

Meanwhile, I was in my village with the rest of my family. At night, many houses were burned down and destroyed. I was afraid, so I spent the nights in the woods with about 15 other boys. My sister, mother, and brother stayed at home.

The people of Ključ are mostly Serbian. Many of the surrounding villages are Muslim. I am Muslim. In some of the villages, particularly in Velegici, hundreds of people were killed. The night I was arrested, I saw dead people in the streets.

After some weeks, we were granted passage to Croatia. We each had to pay 50 German marks to cross the border. That was a lot of money for us. We wrote to the Red Cross that our home in Ramic had been burned down. They gave us food packages in Zagreb and helped in reuniting us with my father and uncle. We lived in Zagreb for three months before my father and uncle were released from the prison camp. During that time, I worked at a construction site, ten hours a day.

When my father and uncle joined us in Zagreb, they were in bad shape. They had suffered dearly in Banja Luka. They had been given one slice of bread a day to share among four people. Many prisoners died of illness and beatings. My father and uncle were both badly beaten. When he came to Zagreb, my father had three broken ribs and open wounds on his nose and head. We spent the rest of our days in Zagreb normally, with no fighting or war.

We left Croatia by bus, traveling first to Vienna. From there we took a plane to Amsterdam, on to New York, and then to Syracuse.

Right now, I spend my days studying English. It's not difficult to learn, because I have studied a foreign language before. I had Russian for six years in school.

I haven't been in Utica long enough to have many impressions. Everything is so new. I have made some friends at my school where I study English. Most of them are refugees from other countries.

Nationally, I consider myself a Bosnian, even though the concept "Bosnian" doesn't exist anymore for many people of my country. Before the war, I lived and spoke with people of different religions and nationalities. We were all living together, Muslims, Croats, and Serbs.

What I want most for myself is to learn English, graduate from high school, and get a job. What I want most for Bosnia is to be free and united. I don't want the country to be divided. Someday I want to go back. I miss Bosnia. I miss the people and how they were before the war.◆

The 1984 Winter Olympic Games were held in Sarajevo. Nineteen-year-old Sandra
Dubravcic, a Yugoslavian figure skater, lit the Olympic flame.

Lamija, eighteen, comes from Mostar, Bosnia-Herzegovina's second-largest city. Lamija's father is a major political figure in the country where he represents the Muslim party.

Lamija describes what it's like being the daughter of a politician in a country at war and how her family's safety is constantly in jeopardy. When a person comes to the United States as a refugee, he or she often seeks political asylum. Asylum means a place where one is safe. And, in Lamija's case, her need for safety is strongly felt.

LAMIJA
THREATS ON MY FATHER'S LIFE

My name is Lamija. I am from Mostar. I came to Boise, Idaho, five months ago as an exchange student. My family is still in Bosnia and Croatia. My mother lives with a friend in Croatia, and my older brother goes to college there. My father goes back and forth a lot between the two countries.

I lived in Croatia as a refugee for a year before I came here. I was living with a family friend, so I really didn't feel like a refugee. I left Mostar because my parents were afraid for me. I didn't want to go. I was 16 at the time. My mom said to me, "I don't want you to feel all of this and remember it all your life, so go ahead and go." I only experienced the actual war in Bosnia for about two months.

Approximately 2.7 million Bosnians fled from danger and persecution in their native land. Two young refugees at a camp in Doksy, Czech Republic are pictured above.

I talk to my mom on the phone, because there is peace in Croatia and I can get through. She lives in a small town called Vrgorac. It's close to Mostar, even though it's in another country. When I was living there, my father traveled a lot between Bosnia and Vrgorac.

He is a politician. He's a pretty important figure in Bosnia right now. That's another reason my parents sent me out of town. Being a politician is dangerous.

My father was president of the Muslim Political Party for Herzegovina. He was quite close to the president of Bosnia, Alija Izetbegovic. Sometimes threats were made on my father's life. He is a really optimistic man and he believes in life, so he never talked about it much. Every time he went out he would have at least two people walking with him.

My mother is a professor of chemistry. She used to teach in the military school. The school was mostly Serb. When my father started in politics, they began hassling her at the school, so she had to leave. Then she started teaching at a high school in Mostar.

My father has been a politician ever since the Communist system began to break down. Before that, he used to have his own company. He always worked for himself, because he never trusted communism. He's really smart, and he's a good scientist. But because he didn't believe in the system, the country never really supported him.

He has strong hopes for Bosnia-Herzegovina. He is a very optimistic man. He never talks about bad things. When we were still living in Mostar and the bombing would last all day long, he would come home from work at eleven or twelve o'clock at night, and I would talk to him. I was so afraid of the war, but he would put hope back into my life. I don't understand how he can be like that with all the things he goes through.

I'm not sure what I'm going to do at this point. I have a wonderful opportunity to stay here. Because I am Bosnian, I can get full asylum in the United States. That would be really good for me, because I could go to college. But then I really miss my family and I want to see them. I can go to college in Croatia if I want, because they have peace there.

It's a dilemma for me. If I stay here, I have some good chances. I'm a really good student; I could make something of my life, achieve something. But if I go back I would be with my family. They won't come here, because my father is committed to Bosnia and my mother doesn't want to leave. It will be a hard choice for me when I do decide where to go. I don't think my family will ever go back to Mostar. Our town is totally destroyed, leveled. There is nothing there.

I like the United States pretty much. It was kind of hard at the beginning, all the new people and everything. But now I have some pretty good friends, and that makes me feel better.

Canadian soldiers serve lunch to children in the Serb-controlled village of Ilijas.

Sometimes people here can be annoying because they don't even know where Bosnia is. Or they ask me stupid questions like, "Do you have candy in Bosnia? Do you have houses?" Most American teenagers don't understand that we had absolutely the same life they do.

I like my school and I am doing well. Not long ago there was a speech contest at Boise State University, and I represented my school. I won third place, and I'm a foreigner!

Sometimes it's hard being here alone. I live with a host family, and I get along with them pretty well, but it's not like being at home. I'll stay in Boise until the end of the school year and then I'll decide what to do next. I would like to go to college and study design or architecture.◆   41

Natasa, a Serb, left Bosnia-Herzegovina without her family when she was seventeen years old. She had just finished her junior year in high school. She now lives in Chicago, Illinois, where she is studying business. Although she plans to stay in the United States until she graduates, Natasa says that she would love to return to her native country and work there if it becomes economically and politically stable.

NATASA
THE "LOST GENERATION"

I came to the United States by myself unlike many other refugees who came here with their families. I was frightened of this new life where I didn't have my parents to help me if I needed them or anyone else to rely on. I often felt alone and lost. It was hard to find the strength and hope to keep on going in life.

The majority of my generation was displaced by the war. They call us the "lost generation." American teenagers should appreciate the life they have, take advantage of the opportunities given to them, and respect each other. So many people take these things for granted. For example, in high school, some people worried about how their hair looked, while I feared for my family's safety and my own uncertain future. People sometimes become too wrapped up in their own worlds and lose sight of what is happening in the world around them.

It was very hard for me to watch what was happening to my "little country" on the news every evening. I would often go to bed crying. It is extremely painful to see your country being torn apart and not be able to influence the situation in any way. It is the same country that gave us life, a childhood, unique memories and lifelong friend-ships. And now we're being told that it doesn't exist anymore, that we have no country, and nowhere to go. I don't want to believe that. We all want to return to the good old times again, we want a sense of belonging and sense of direction. If we only knew the right path to take.

I grew up in a multicultural country where I never hated anyone because of their religion. But it was hard listening to the American media which focused mainly on Serb atrocities, even though we all know that in any war all sides are guilty of wrongdoing. Unfortunately, Americans who are not familiar with the history of the region and details of this conflict are influenced by this biased view.

Many people do not know about the Serb victims of the war. These people had nowhere to go except Serbia, which already has a large refugee population. Since Serbs were seen as the aggressors in the civil war, it was more difficult for them to obtain refugee status in foreign countries. As refugees they would be allowed to live and work in other countries legally.

The Balkan region has always been in the midst of conflict and almost every generation has gone through or at least been touched by war. My generation was in total disbelief when civil war broke out on April 6, 1992, in Sarajevo. We were certain that the ethnic tensions were only temporary and would eventually settle down.

Unfortunately, that did not prove to be the case. This war took away the best years of our lives. We had to grow up too fast and skip the innocent years of laughter and joy. I remember being scared and my parents telling me not to worry even though I knew that they were scared as well and didn't know what would happen. We all wanted to live in the world of dolls and childishness and not in this cruel world of war, blood, and suffering.

As teenage immigrants we go through a lot, we learn to fight for ourselves and for our future. I think that this experience makes us stronger individuals and enriches our personalities on both intellectual and psychological levels. We cannot afford to lose our hopes or fail when facing an obstacle.◆

Esmir, a Muslim, comes from Mostar, the chief city of Herzegovina. He has a keen sense of events and their significance in the war. He is very methodical in his thinking and views his country from a complex historical perspective.

Esmir is intelligent and strong-willed. Beneath his cool exterior lies great anguish and rage about his father, who was badly wounded in the war. Esmir's self-confidence helps keep his family together.

ESMIR
A GUN AT MY HEAD

My name is Esmir. I live in Jacksonville, Florida. I came here from Mostar two months ago with my mother and my sister, Emza.

There was a big explosion in Mostar on April 6, 1992. All the buildings within 50 meters were damaged or destroyed. The Croats were responsible for the explosion. At that time, the military in Mostar was controlled by the Serbs; many of the soldiers were Serbs.

The first shooting in Mostar happened around April 10. It was nothing compared to those that came later. At first, I was so afraid that I couldn't sleep at night. Later, people got used to it; there was shooting all night and no one cared.

Mostar is in Herzegovina, in a valley of the Neretva River. It is completely surrounded by mountains and hills. Like all cities in Bosnia, Mostar was very cosmopolitan. Muslims, Serbs, and Croats all lived together. There was also a small group of Jews. Before the war, Mostar's population was 150,000. It was the second-largest city in Bosnia-Herzegovina, after Sarajevo. Now only 40,000 people live there.

When the war started, the Croats controlled the area on the right, or eastern, bank of the Neretva, which was mostly Muslim. The Serbs occupied all the hills around the east side of the city. The Muslims on the western bank had very few arms, and it took the Serbs only fifteen days to conquer that part of the city. The west bank fell on June 15, 1992.

Our house was on the west side. On July 20, 1992, the Muslims and Croats led a big offensive and managed to liberate a tiny strip of land along the western bank. That was how we lived for one year.

On May 9, 1993, the second war, between the Muslims and the Croats, broke out and we were no longer allies. The eastern bank and parts of the western bank just along the Neretva were held by Muslims, but there were also 20,000 Muslims living in Croat-held parts. My house was right on the front line between these territories. I could look out on the front line from our living room. Eventually, the building I lived in was destroyed.

When the second war started, my father was wounded by an antiaircraft grenade that was fired into our apartment building. The big bullet went through the wall down to the floor, bounced back up through the door and into the hallway through a wooden chair my father was sitting on. It swept

Mostar's "old bridge," built in the sixteenth century during Turkish rule, spans the Neretva River. In November, 1993, the stone footbridge was shelled and severely damaged by Croat forces.

through the bottom part of both his thighs, and the chair shattered. All the little splinters of wood went into his legs. He got blood poisoning.

It was hard to get him to the hospital, because all the hospitals were on the Croat-held side. Six days later, he was transported to a provisional hospital on the western bank, but they had no medication. When the Bosnian Army arrived, he was taken to a hospital on the eastern bank. He didn't get the surgery he needed until 15 days after being wounded. After spending two months in Mostar, my father was transported to a hospital in Zagreb, Croatia. Life for Muslims on the western bank was very difficult. There were about 20,000 of us on the west side of the river, and about 50,000 were in camps.

Refugees on a makeshift raft transport a car across the Neretva River.

One day the Croats tried to seize our building. There had been shooting all day, and we had to go down to the shelter in the basement because all the windows faced the Croat side. You couldn't move your head for fear of being shot by snipers.

I am 17, but I look older. My mother was often afraid for me. The Croat soldiers came into the shelter with guns. When a soldier asked me my name, I said, "Esmir Celebic." Then he asked, "Are you Muslim?" "Yes," I answered. All the while, he was pointing a gun right at my head. My mother was clutching my arm. Then he asked me if I was in the Bosnian Army, and my mother said, "Oh no! He's only sixteen years old!" My sister and I always tease her about how dramatic she is.

One day a boy from the Bosnian Army sneaked
into the building and found us. He asked if we

wanted to go to another part of town that was held by Muslims, a neighborhood called Cernica. This was all happening while my father was in the hospital; we had no idea how he was doing. To get across to Cernica, we had to cross a bridge.

Mostar had five bridges. During the first part of the war, the Serbs mined all the bridges in Mostar except the old stone bridge, built in 1566.

One day the old bridge was opened up to those who wanted to go to the east. That's when my mother, my sister, and I left. A few days later, it was closed again and we couldn't go back. We stayed with my aunt, my father's sister, on the east side.

The streets were filled with soldiers. Every night they would look into the houses and search all the apartments. They were looking for arms and for men. Any men over eighteen years were taken to the camps. We knew we had to leave.

The day I left Mostar, I went to my grandparents' house in a neighborhood called Brankovac to say goodbye. Brankovac was a famous Serbian poet from Mostar. He wrote during this century and was famous because he wanted Serbs and Muslims to be friends. The Turks had ruled Bosnia for 500 years. In the current war, the Serbs want to kill anyone who is a Muslim. It is their revenge.

UN officials transported us out of Mostar. We went to Croatia. In Split, we applied to the International Rescue Committee for help, and now here I am in Jacksonville. My father is still in Zagreb. He's out of the hospital now and coming here soon.

My father is a professor of history. He taught at the University of Mostar. His field involved cultural societies of Mostar from 1900 to 1950. He was also the curator of the archives of Herzegovina. My mother used to do electrical drawings for buildings. She worked at that job for 22 years and then was fired because she was Muslim.

Before the war, I never felt any tensions between people. We had friends who were Croats and Serbs. People didn't care what you were. After World War II, when Yugoslavia was created, the only way to keep the peace was to forget about nationalities.

I'm a senior in high school here. I'm the best in my class in Latin. Americans can't say some words in Latin, so when I say them all my classmates are amazed. I got an A in calculus two weeks after we got here. At that time I was six weeks behind, so I think that's pretty good.

I like my school here in the United States. I have made some new friends. I don't want to go back to Bosnia. I no longer have a home there. I don't have anything there. My whole family is here except for an aunt who is still in Sarajevo. None of my friends are there. Many of them will never go back. Mostar is dead now.◆

A man cycles by the remains of vehicles destroyed by heavy fighting in central Sarajevo. Sniper fire often prevented parts of the city from being cleaned up.

Naida comes from Sarajevo, Bosnia-Herzegovina's major city. Before the war, life in Sarajevo was like that of many urban centers. People enjoyed the libraries, the museums, the cinemas, and the theater.

Sarajevo is the cultural dividing line between major religious and ethnic worlds. Before the war, many Sarajevans demonstrated a remarkable desire for integration. Many Sarajevans were proud of this accomplishment, and, like Naida, wanted it to grow. But the war in Bosnia has swept away the dynamic aspects of integration.

Naida spends a great deal of time thinking about the plight of her country. She has written about the war for *Newsweek* and has appeared on panels and at conferences around the country. She bears the intense pain of her shattered city and country with amazing strength and keen political insight.

NAIDA
A WAR FOR POWER

My name is Naida. I was born and raised in Sarajevo. I came to the United States in 1991 as a foreign exchange student. That was before the war broke out in Yugoslavia.

I am here by myself. My family is still in Sarajevo, my older brother and my mother. My father died four years ago. About every two months I get a letter from home. I don't know if they're getting enough food. I can only hope.

They won't come to the U.S. My mother is 55, and I don't think she would be willing to move. She is a doctor and works in a hospital in Sarajevo.

I just finished my freshman year at Western Maryland College in Westminster. I'm studying math on a four-year scholarship. It pays for my tuition, but I have to make money for room and board.

I work a lot right now, during summer vacation, in Essex, a suburb of Baltimore, where I live with a host family. I work 65 to 70 hours a week to save money to support myself next year at school. I'm a technical assistant at Johns Hopkins University. I help graduate students in the mechanical engineering lab. At night and on weekends I work as a hostess in a restaurant in Essex. It's a chain restaurant, not great, but okay. I get tired a lot.

I don't like living in the suburbs. It's really flat, boring, gray. I hate it that I need a car just to buy food. It's a ten-minute drive to the grocery store.

I like the area around my college better. There's a lot of greenery and hills. It looks like home. It's strange how much that means.

I saw the separation among the people of Bosnia starting about a year before the war broke out. Some people say they were preparing for war even ten years ago. I never thought Yugoslavians were preparing for war.

The rise in nationalism was a surprise to me. It was never present in me, or in my friends, and it never will be. I guess it was my generation that was most surprised by the war.

The problem in Yugoslavia is not that it is a religious war, as many people would like to think. It's a war for power. Certain factions have complete control of the press and the media. What you see on television in Serbia is totally different from what you see in Bosnia-Herzegovina or Croatia. They make the people in the villages believe it's a

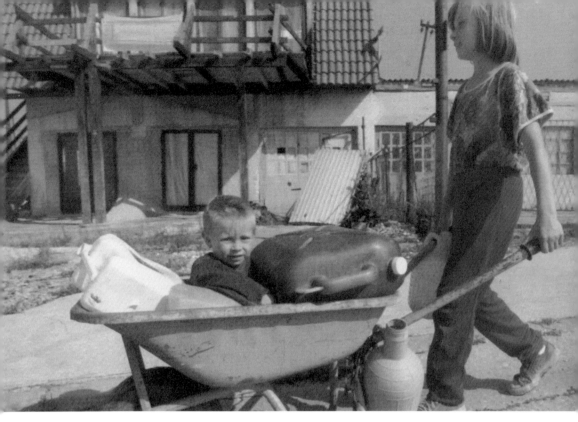

A Bosnian girl and her brother fetch water for their family in Sarajevo. The city was under siege for nearly four years and was without water much of the time.

religious war. If this was a war about nationality and religion, Croatia and Serbia wouldn't be making deals.

Bosnia was an integrated land. Forty percent of the people in Sarajevo have mixed marriages. It's less mixed in the country, but I never saw deep hatred between people there. The power lies with a handful of people. A lot of what they say is propaganda.

As far as nationality is concerned, I don't regard myself as anything, nor do I have any religious beliefs. I like to think of myself as an internationalist.

In Yugoslavia, people had a more relaxed way of being religious. My parents are both Muslims,

During the war, hundreds of cultural monuments and places of worship in Bosnia-Herzegovina were destroyed. Pictured above are people at work on the reconstruction of a mosque in Mostar after the war.

but not really religious. I guess they believed, but in a relaxed way.

In the fall I will go back to school in Westminster. I have to say, I think American college students are less serious than Bosnians. They only know about life in the U.S., nothing outside it. Maybe it's because they have parents and a home here. Because I'm a foreigner and alone, I have to take care of myself.

I am very angry at the international community's response to the war in Bosnia. It has been very passive. For two years, it has been clear how much aggression is going on and who is doing it, yet the world community does nothing. I feel the world is responsible.

So far, I've been disappointed by the actions taken here to stop the war. At a rally I went to in Washington, D.C., the people who attended were religiously oriented. There were Muslims, Christians, and Jews. That's not the way to solve the situation.

You don't solve this problem with religion or ethnicity, but by being human. Sometimes people seem to think I'm crazy, but I have many friends, all of different ethnicities and religions, who feel as I do. That is what gives me hope. ◆

Glossary

atrocity An act of extreme cruelty or brutality.

Balkans The countries of the Balkan Peninsula in Europe. These countries include Albania, Bosnia-Herzegovina, Bulgaria, Croatia, Greece, Macedonia, Romania, Slovenia, Turkey, and Yugoslavia (made up of the former republics of Serbia and Montenegro). This region has been a center of political unrest for centuries.

charisma A special charm or appeal, often inspiring admiration and loyalty.

civil war A war between citizens of the same country.

communism A political system in which economic resources are owned by the government rather than by individuals.

concentration camp A place where prisoners are held, often under severe conditions.

diplomacy The relations and negotiations between nations.

ethnic cleansing The attempt by one ethnic group to remove all other ethnic groups from a region or country, often through military force.

ethnic group A large group of people who share common racial, national, cultural, religious, or linguistic characteristics.

federation A group of territories governed by a central authority. Each territory within the federation has limited powers to govern itself and the country as a whole.

Islam The religion of the Muslims, whose God is Allah and whose holy book is the Koran.

migrate To move from one country or place to another.

nationalism A sense of national pride that places the interests of one nation over those of all other nations; excessive patriotism.

persecute To harass a group of people because of its race, religion, nationality, or ethnicity.

propaganda Information or rumors that are deliberately spread to promote a cause or to hurt another cause.

rally To join together in a common cause or purpose.

refugee Person who flees to another country to escape from war or persecution.

sanction The breaking off of economic and military ties with a nation in order to punish it for not respecting international law.

stoicism Not showing emotion or feelings, especially when faced with pain or distress.

tolerance A fair and accepting attitude toward persons of a race, nationality, or religion other than one's own.

For Further Reading

Andric, Ivo. *The Bridge on the Drina*. Chicago: University of Chicago Press, 1977.

Colakovic, Branko. *Yugoslav Migrations to America*. San Fransisco: R and E Research Associates, 1973.

Dizdarevic, Zlatko. *Sarajevo: A War Journal*. New York: Henry Holt, 1994.

Djilas, Aleksa. *Contested Country*. Cambridge: Harvard University Press, 1991.

Dragnich, Alex. *Serbs and Croats: The Struggle in Yugoslavia*. New York: Harcourt, Brace, Jovanovich, 1992.

Drakulic, Slavenka. *Balkan Express: Fragments from the Other Side of War*. New York: Norton, 1993.

Filipovic, Zlata. *Zlata's Diary*. New York: Viking, 1994.

Glenny, Misha. *The Fall of Yugoslavia: The Third Balkan War*. New York: Penguin, 1994.

Kaplan, Robert. *Balkan Ghosts: A Journey Through History*. New York: St. Martin's Press, 1993.

Thompson, Mark. *Paper House: The Ending of Yugoslavia*. New York: Pantheon, 1992.

Index

ABOUT THE AUTHOR
Valerie Tekavec is a freelance writer and translator. She teaches English courses at Bard College and lives in Woodstock, New York.

PHOTO CREDITS
p. 9 © REUTERS/Charles Platiau/Archive Photos; pp. 14, 30 © Valerie Tekavec; p. 25 © REUTERS/Peter Andrews/Archive Photos; p. 38 © Sean Sprague/Impact Visuals; p. 42 © REUTERS/Corinne Dufka/Archive Photos; p. 49 © Dominique Barbesino/Impact Visuals; all other photos © AP/Wide World Photos.

LAYOUT AND DESIGN
Kim Sonsky